W9-AZS-189

Published and distributed in the United States by:
Hay House, Inc. P.O. Box 5100,
Carlsbad, CA 92018-5100
(800) 654-5126 • (800) 650-5115 (fax)

Book design: Jenny Richards

1-56170-669-8
02 01 00 99   4 3 2 1
First Printing, December 1999

Printed in the United States of America